THE ADVENTURES OF LITTLE JAM
THE SKATEPARK

by Jamison Phillips & Patrick Phillips, MSW
Illustrated by Cameron Wilson

TheAdventuresOfLittleJam@gmail.com
MrPhillipsTheChangeAgent@gmail.com
Library of Congress Control Number: 2018901236
ISBN-13:978-1985764941
10:1985764946
Educational Empowerment Group, LLC First Edition

Jam and his dad Patrick were riding their bikes on the trail when they saw something amazing.

"Dad look a skatepark!"

Jam and his dad rode their bikes closer to get a better look at the skatepark. Jam could not believe what he saw.

The skaters at the park were doing amazing tricks.

"Dad do you see that? He just slid down the rail?"

"Oh my goodness dad, he just jumped out the bowl!"

"Dad he just rode all the way up the wall!"

Jam looked at his dad with such excitement and said, "I want a skateboard dad!"

Jam's dad did not know what to say because he had never ridden a skateboard and knew very little about skateboards.

The next day Jam and his dad visited a local skate shop and they could not believe what they saw. There were so many different types of skateboards, long boards, penny boards and street boards. Jam and his dad looked around for a while before buying two skateboards, helmets and pads.

CITY SKATEBOA
17
Eleme
580NYC
Flibl

"I can't wait to ride my board dad," Jam said as they walked out the skate shop.

SKATE SHOP

The next day Jam and his dad went to the skatepark. Jam was so excited to ride his new skateboard with the other skaters.

"This is so cool!"

Jam eagerly strapped on his helmet and jumped on his board, then something happened...

SPLATT! BOOM BOOM!

Jam fell flat on his back. "Ouch my bottom hurts dad!" Jam yelled.

Jam stumbled back to his feet and stood back on his skateboard and fell backwards again.

His legs flew high in the air and he fell on his side, "ouch I fell again dad!"

SPLATT! BOOM BOOM!

Jam began crying and said, "I don't like this skateboard!"

Jam's dad wobbled onto his board to show Jam how to skate. Jam's dad opened his arms wide and slowly placed one foot
after the other on the board, when
"Splat Boom Boom," he fell to the ground.

Jam and his dad were starting to realize that skateboarding was not as easy as it looked.

Jam and his dad came up with a master plan. They decided to go home and watch videos about skateboarding to learn the basics.

While at home watching skate videos Jam and his dad learned so much about riding goofy footed or regular stance, how to stand and balance while on the board, how to kick push, how to turn and carve on a skateboard and how to stop a skateboard.

The next day Jam and his dad returned to the skatepark confident and ready to skate.

Jam and his dad strapped on helmets and pads and jumped on their skateboards when something happened.

While on his board, Jam did not fall this time. Jam's perseverance had paid off. Jam and his dad rode around on their skateboards leaning and turning their skateboards for hours, but there was one challenge they must overcome before leaving the skatepark.

ZOOOM! WHIZ!!!! ZIP!

Before leaving the skatepark, Jam and his dad wanted to conquer a new challenge by riding down one of the banks. Jam and his dad rode over to the bank and while it was not that tall, the fear of falling while going down the ramp made the ramp seem like it was tall as the Empire State Building.

After a few moments of contemplating going down the ramp, Jam's dad decided to give it a try. Jam's dad stepped onto his board, opened his arms wide like an airplane, and wobbled down the ramp looking like a baby learning to walk.

Now it was Jam's turn, but he was too scared to go down. Jam's dad encouraged Jam and told him that he could make it. After a few moments Jam decided to ride down the ramp.
Jam thought to himself;

Step 1, raise your arms like an airplane...

Step 2, bend your knees for balance...

Step 3, place one foot on the skateboard...

Step 4, give the skateboard a good push off

and go!

ZOOOM! WHIZ!!!!! ZIP!

"I did it dad, I made it down the ramp!" Jam's dad gave him a high five as they celebrated their victory over the ramp.

"You see son, you can do anything that you put your mind to. In life you will face many challenges, sometimes they are in the form of ramps at the skatepark and sometimes they are overcoming your fear of trying new things or learning something new in school. The key is that you face your fears, never quit and always do your best."

With a sense of accomplishment Jam and his dad hopped on their boards and skated back to the car.

"I love you dad."

 "I love you too son."

Skating was not so hard anymore.

CONNECT WITH US

theadventuresoflittlejam.com

 @theadventuresoflittlejam

 @theadventuresoflittlejam

 @theadventuresoflittlejam

mrphillipsthechangeagent.com

 @MrPhillipsTheChangeAgent

 @mrphillipsthechangeagent

 @mrphillipsthechangeagent